tears of silence

photographs by
donna moyseuik

editorial consultants
linda macdonald, margaret ordway,
daniel mcdonald and flavio belli

designed by
michel socha

tears of silence

By *JEAN VANIER*
(author of "in weakness, strength")

griffin house
toronto 1970

isbn 0 88760 005 0

published by griffin press limited
455 king street west, toronto, canada   M5V 1K7

first published 1970
second printing 1971
third printing 1972
fourth printing 1973

I would like to thank especially Donna, Linda
and Flavio who worked so hard to make this
book possible.

JEAN VANIER

printed and bound in canada by
THE ALGER PRESS LIMITED

Our lives are fleeting moments in which are found the seeds
of eternal peace, unity and love as well as the seeds of war,
dissension and indifference. When will we rise and awaken
to the choice before each of us, to water and to give light
to one or the other of these two seeds?
Must we accept damnation or can humanity be saved?

This book is dedicated to all those of the House of the Dying
in Calcutta. It is dedicated to the faces that are shown here,
faces and people who represent you and me, and all those
who are fearful, and all those who aspire to universal
brotherhood.

I grieve to speak of love and yet not love as I should.
I ask forgiveness of the many I have wounded
and of the many I have passed without seeing their wounds.
Pray for me, my brother.

How many times
        a meeting has struck barriers
            cement blocks
                in me
heart of stone
heart of stone
        unable to listen
           i fear
          and fly by
who can liberate me from myself?

he who clutches desperately to security —
     to every day habits, work, organization, friends,
                                      family. . . . .

           closed off . . . .

      no longer lives:

      more than security,

          life needs

                    adventure

                    risk

                    dynamic activity

                    self-giving

                    presence to others

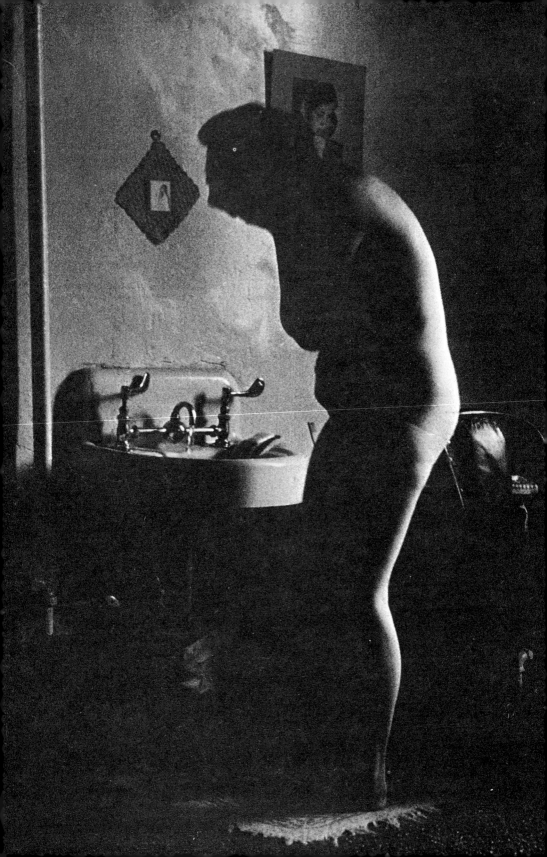

in the paths of our existence

there are at times obstacles . . . . . .

rocks barring the road . . . . . .

if these obstacles appear too great

or if we, through fatigue or other reasons,

are deflated,

then we sit and weep

unable to advance . . . . . unable to
return . . . . .

some failure has damaged our
élan . . . .

an unfaithful friend

failure in exams

in work

we no longer feel that blossoming dynamism

we carry our bodies like lumps of lead,

lumps of lead,

we slumber into a world of disillusionment

apathetic
listless

but then comes change

winter changes to spring

we meet a friend

we rest

forces awaken in our bodies

life seems to surge once more . . . .

as the morning sun

calm
unswerving
certain
never faltering

. . . . .others fall,

        sink into sadness,

        rise

        but fall again too quickly. . . . . .

        obstacle seems to follow obstacle

and they remain deflated. . . .depressed. . . .downhearted. . . .

        crushed

    life does not seem to blossom. . . . . .

        the joy of living has fled

        maybe never was

from depression

        they are sucked into despair

from sadness

        into misery

. . . .alone

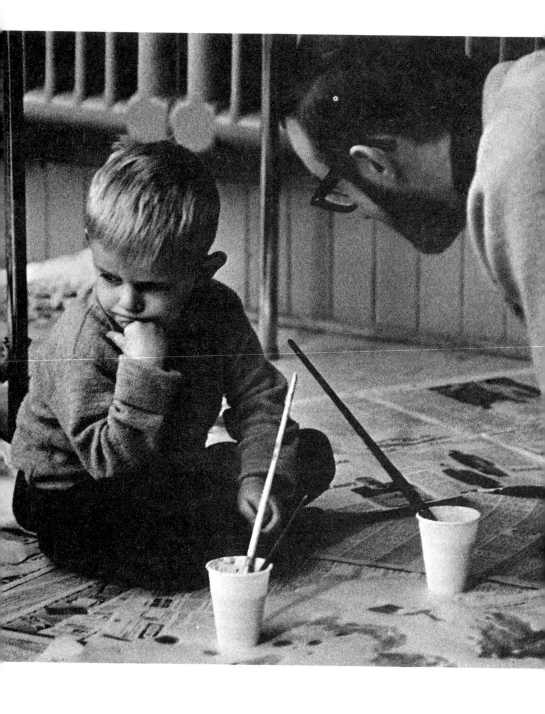

the man in misery is crushed. . . . . encircled

without hope of rising by himself

surrounded and knotted with obstacles and
difficulties. . . . .

no desire

no hope

no motivation

no will to live

closed off

man is a marvelous and mysterious being

when called forth

calling forth

strength

tenderness

can surge up in him

giving life

and then there can be a bursting forth of quiet energy. . . . . .
capacity for creativity. . . . . . generosity. . . . . . deep
attention. . . . . . concern. . . . . . work. . . . . . a sense of
wonderment. . . . . . some taste of the infinite. . .
never ceasing. . . . evolving. . . . deepening. . .
creating. . . . . . calling. . . . . .

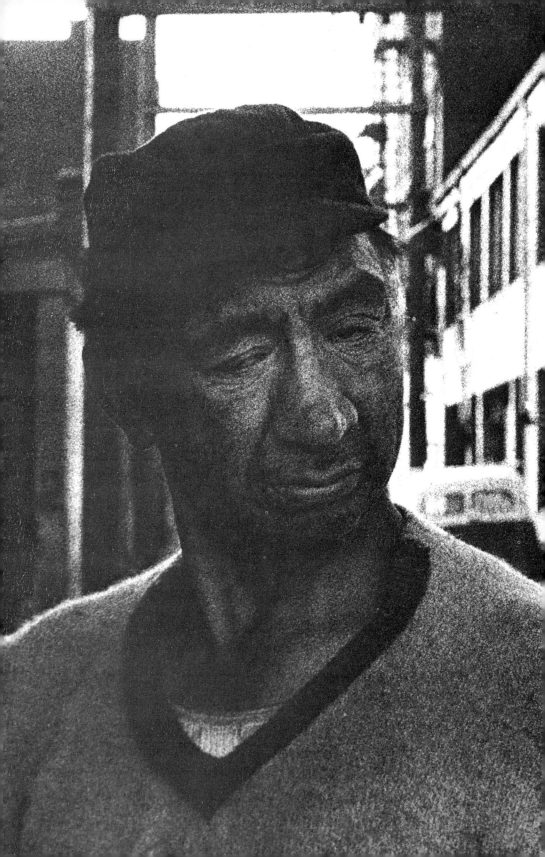

when something interests me
how easy it becomes
vital . . . . . living
no interest . . . . . apathy
i wander down life's path
cynical
and sad
sad unto death
how quickly i die
who will call me forth?

being down......with no life
no beauty
that beauty which flows with life......
eyes....
living eyes...
not radiating
no longer a source of attraction....
nothing in me attracts....
people turn away their eyes.....
i am not only dejected
but rejected
covered with shame
deserted...abandoned...
alone.....in anguish
crucified

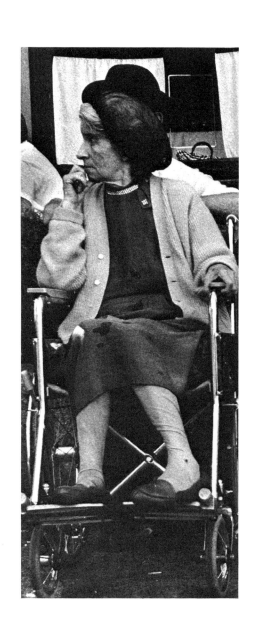

i who am dejected
        let go that inner hold......
                sink down......down.....
    friends drift downstream
                    laughing....
i remain......lying on my bed
          smoking
          drinking
        or sitting....sitting
         the radio playing on and on and on
        waiting
        waiting
         but waiting for
            what.....

and i am afraid......

        those haggard eyes

           or open wounds

           or black skin or white skin

           or alcoholic smell

           or freaked out mind

                of the man in misery

        strike deep chords of fear within me....

    fear of losing my money, time, reputation, liberty

      fear, above all, of losing myself

        fear of the unknown,

            for misery is a world of the unknown.....

        terror of despair,

             those hands.... those hands.....

              those hands stretched out towards
                                  me....

              i am afraid to touch them......

                they may drag me down, down,

                  down to some unknown
                        future........

i fear my helplessness
       my hollows
             my poverty

you remind me that i too must die

and so i turn my back
       returning to my home
             escaping the fundamental reality
                of my own existence,
                   of my own poverty
                      and yours, my brother. . . . .
               i refuse to love. . . . . .

because i fear your grasping hand

        calling me to the unknown

          the unknown of love

because i fear my emptiness

      my poverty

      my call to death

    i fear myself

    i close my heart.....cement block...

      shut myself off

      from you,

        my despairing brother

you are in a prison of despair, sadness...

i too am in prison

  but my bars and locks

    are my so-called friends, clubs, social conventions,

      "what everybody else is doing"...

barriers that i have built

    that prevent me seeing you,

      my brother

your presence,

    miserable, sad...

      is a call....

        do i turn away

          or do i dare.....

love is the greatest of all risks

    to give myself....to you

    do i dare....do i dare

        leap into the cool, swirling, living waters

      of loving fidelity

.....the miserable man is still there
    waiting...waiting....waiting for what
        lying in his prison....
        lying in his dung.....
          waiting
          yet
          not waiting
          for he has lost hope
we only wait when there is hope
where there is no hope......we lie.....dying
    not living
    sad unto death
    yet he waits
        waiting.............yet not waiting

the worthy lady, over rimmed glasses, saying:

    "lazy"

the bank manager shouting:

    "stupid"

are right. . . .in a way. . . .

the miserable man knows it only too well

his misery is the awareness of his misery

    "i remain in the vomit of my worthlessness. . . . ."

he knows this worthlessness

    and has lost hope

the man in misery is not ignorant

only lacking in strength. . . .vitality

that which springs from hope

       and he has no hope. . . . . .

his misery is greater because of his awareness

      therein lies his despair

      he cannot rise

      not feeling worthy to rise

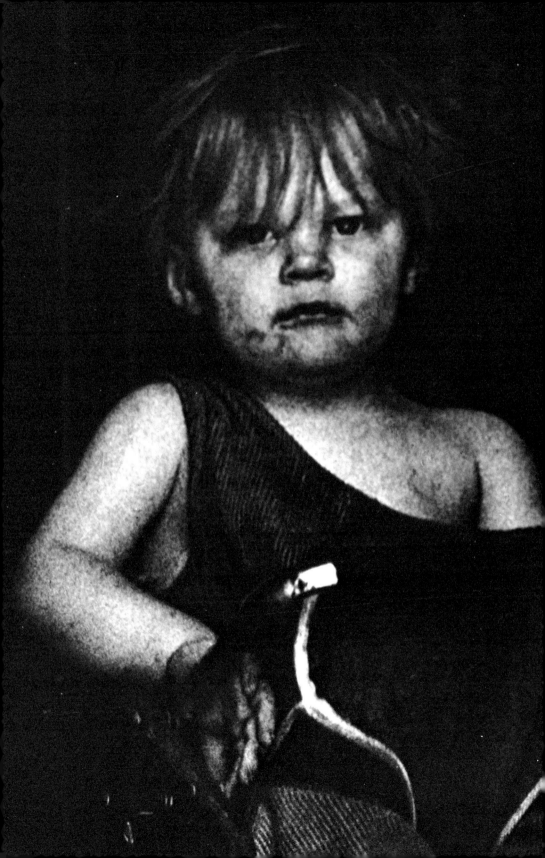

the person in misery does not need a look that
        judges and criticizes
    but a comforting presence
        that brings peace and hope and life
        and says:
            "you are a human person
                important
                mysterious
                infinitely precious
            what you have to say
                is important
                because it flows
                    from a human person
        in you there are those seeds
                of the infinite
                those germs of love. . .of beauty
                which must rise from the earth
                                    of your misery
                so humanity be fulfilled.
        if you do not rise
            then something will be missing
                if you are not fulfilled
                    it is terrible
                    you must rise again
                        on the third day. . . . .
                rise again because we all need
                you
                for you are a child of God
                you, sam
                        john
                                willie mae
                    my brother. . . .my sister
                        be loved
                        beloved"

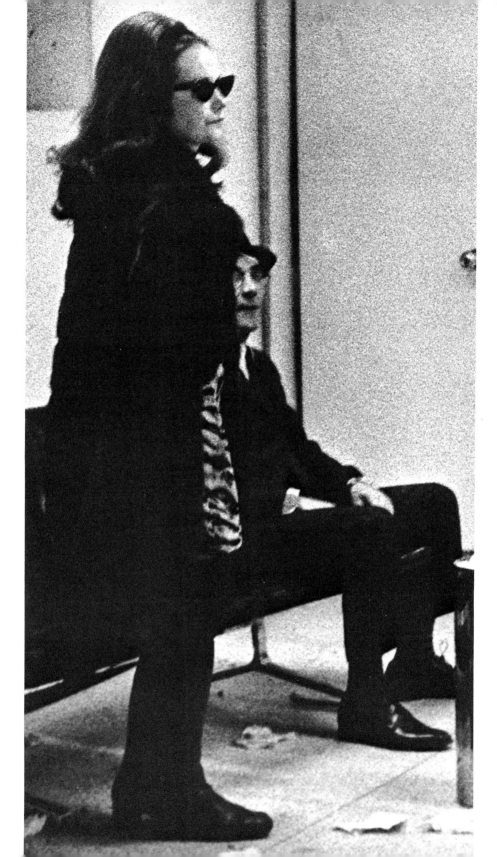

In some mysterious way
        the quality of my presence my look
            brings to you life

        or death

that look......

       that hand......

             calls forth

                    life....hope....joy...

if

you believe in me

then maybe

i can do something worthwhile......

      maybe i am worthwhile

maybe i can do something with my life

thus

the light of hope begins to burn

   your constant trust in me

      communicates warm sensations of confidence

         and faith

     that look in your eyes

       the touch of your hands

          brings me some marvellous message of hope

"your slightest look easily will unclose me
though i have closed myself as fingers,
you open always petal by petal as Spring comes
(touching skilfully, mysteriously) her first
rose"

                  e. e. cummings

how then to approach the miserable child
            not haughtily
                        but humbly
            not judging but loving
                        determined not to dominate
                        not even to give things
                        rather to give myself
                                    my time
                                                energy
                        and heart

and to listen
            believing that he is important
                        a child of God
                                    in whom Jesus lives

approach with tenderness
                        gently

gently giving one's friendship
                        delicate soothing hands
                                    bearing the oil of mercy
                                    annointing deep wounds

"A new heart will I give you
and a new spirit I will put within
you and I will take out of your
flesh the heart of stone and give
you a heart of flesh."
                        (ezechiel 36:26)

he who is

        or has been

           deeply hurt

   has a RIGHT

      to be sure

        he is

       L O V E D

love!

        not just some passing moment
            a glance however open
but some deeper compassion
            radiating permanency
not some morbid curiosity
          some gushing pity
            incompetent naiveté

the cry of burnt-out eyes
            wounded bodies
        addicted minds
          cravings
can only be answered by some deeper love
        in which is felt a strange presence of the eternal
          a hope
          a new security
not some passing glance
        but deeper bonds
          unbreakable

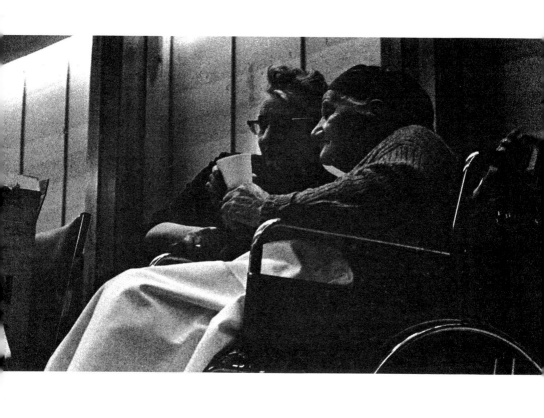

com-passion

is a meaningful word. . . . .

sharing the same passion

the same suffering

the same agony

accepting in my heart

the misery in yours, o, my brother

and you, accepting me

o yes there is fear

but even more deeply

there is the insistent cry from the entrails of the
suffering one

that calls me forth. . . . .

some faint feeling

of confidence

that my smile. . . . . .my presence

has value and can give

life

thus deep friendship is born

mutual presence
humble and forgiving
engendering

quiet joy
fidelity

but

who will bring life to

the despairing,

to crushed and dying hearts

to those whose future is barred

to the mentally sick

to the aged and alone

to the despised and anguished

to the burnt out

statesmen are called upon to enact laws

but who is called to give hope to the despairing

how to approach him

he, repulsive and fearful

i, with my fear and my security

and yet......

i feel.....in some mysterious way

that there is a calling

the silent crying out of misery

tears of silence

and in my deepest being i hear this call

a sort of whispering

that life has meaning, but

in the degree that i find love

no reasons.....no reasons why......only a sort of.....

an act.....

an act of faith that i can enter into some vast and powerful

movement

of life and life giving

. . . . that my joy gives joy

       my hope gives hope

and

      that i can communicate in some silent way

        the spirit living in me

          not by what i say

            but how i say it

       a deep concern

        a way of listening

          to the faint heart beats

            of your existence and life

listening
l i s t e n i n g
l i s t e n i n g
                    whispering
                    silent
                    a listening that comforts
                              and calls forth

DO I DARE
do i dare
      believe
           your silent call
                your tears of silence

but there is the world of efficiency
                         techniques
                         diplomas
                         business (and business is business!)

and then there are my friends
           who think i'm crazy . . . . . are they friends?
                              am i crazy?

. . . . DOUBTS . . . . . .

conflicting forces
           fatigue
           fears

and yet life calls forth
           compassion in my entrails

this strange and silent war
           do i dare
           do i dare
                believe
           do i dare
           do i dare

           surrender myself to your call

"if you pour yourself out for the hungry
  and satisfy the desire of the afflicted
    then shall your light rise in the darkness
      and your gloom be as the noonday
        and the Lord will guide you continually

and you shall be like a watered garden
  like a spring of water
    whose waters fail not."

isaiah 58

o God

   my God

      keep me from flinching/waning

         slumbering into that timeless rest

            that never is

keep me from falling into a prison

              of egotistical habits

            where the bars

            are superficial friends

                and drinks

                and stupid laughter

                kisses without love

                business and organisation

                  without heart

                and gifts for self-flattery

          these bars that prevent life evolving

            towards that taste of the infinite

              open to your call . . . .

break down those barriers

      that prevent me living, my God,

break down those barriers

      that threaten to stifle me . . . .

barriers broken down too quickly

        are

            another form

                of death......

          too much exposure

          too much cold

     those who have learned life too quickly

        have thus lost life

  those who have thrown themselves into

                experiences of sexuality

             drugs for escape

       but who have lost life :

              presence

             communion

        because love grows

           is a deepening fusion of peace

               and liberty

i fear

       the mysterious power of compassion

       i

       do not

       believe in it

because that implies having found myself

       that i no longer play

          play a game

          put on a mask — a personage

          pretending to be

          appearing

       but that i become myself

          accepting my poverty

          letting the Spirit breathe

              move
              live
              love

                 in me

opening my being

          (no fear)

to the delicate touch

of His hand that opens me

       but i fear

       and wear my mask

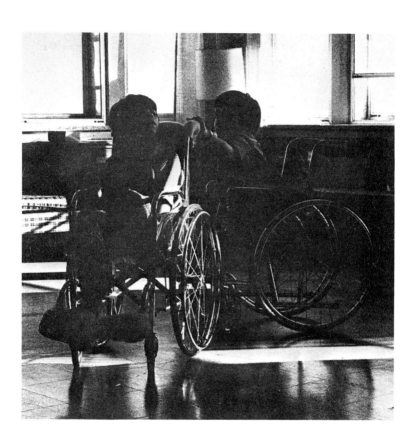

maturity of the heart:
      accepting
      myself
          with my limits
          in my poverty
          i do not fear
               the
               other

no fear that
          i will be eaten up
          devoured
          lose my being

no fear
      of showing who i am

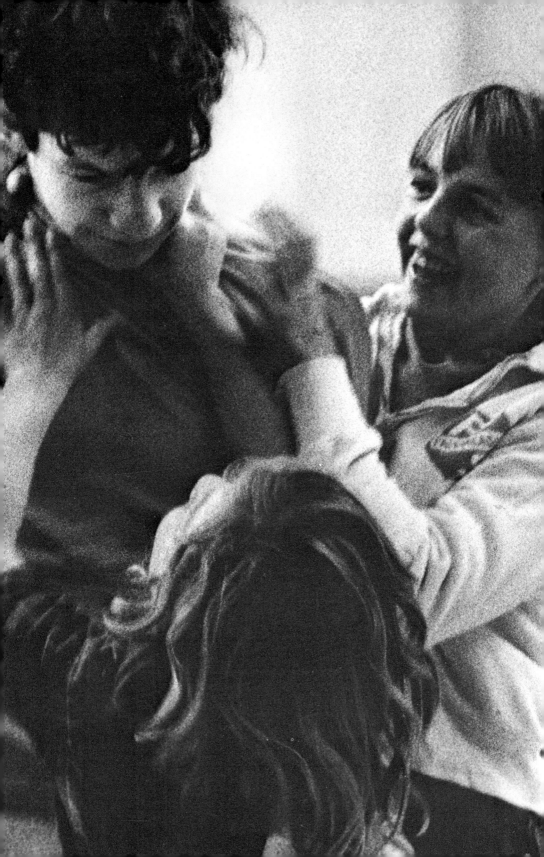

in each of us there is a need to

L I V E

the flowering out of life
the thirst for beautiful things

the feel of my radiance
in joy
in hope

in each of us there is a need to live

        but also

there are those seeds of death

        no will to live

        no desire to get up in the morning

        never able to sleep . . . . always wanting
                            to sleep . . . . .

        but never sleeping

        always down

           and criticizing

        no zest or energy

        just-every-day-doing-what-i-must

           with no zing

               or laughter

i need to feel

        i am

        i am unique

            capable of love and life

                not just one of the crowd

                    looking towards life

                      but myself living. . . . .

i must not remain in a sort of

                      non-life

                      non-existence

                      closed in

                      despairing

        for this can be a taste of death. . . . .

life is a flowering vine.....

        too much light......or too little

        too much water......or too little

brings blight and death....burnt-up, dried up, drowned......

life needs delicate gentle hands, hands that know
just the right amount of water for life
just the right degree of light
at the right time....

or else, no life, no flower, no fruit.......

to evolve

      life does need security

           in the mother

           in the father

           in the home

               with friends

      but above all trust in the spirit

           against all assaults of fear and anguish

           against all the unknowns

           against anything that might destroy

               the flowering of my life...

the biological movement

        of growth

        needs

this physical and spiritual

        complement of love

      and so to evolve

      the child

      needs

     the look

     the hands

       of his mother

life needs

        security and hope

security being
the fundamental basis

        the earth

          in which life is born

hope being
that call . . . . . to light

        and love

         and beauty

       . . . . . . universality

        shadows of the infinite

                        risk
                        and hope
            love of the unknown
            passionate interest in the present

            thirst for adventure
            desire for new experiences

            outpourings of generosity
            quest for knowledge
            openness to the future
            call to love
            availability to the Spirit
            peaceful contemplation
                                    high skies
                                    mountains
                                    deep lakes
                                    deep breathing
                                    wonderment

love is the greatest of all risks

       the giving of myself

but do i dare take this risk
       diving into the cool
       swirling
       living waters of

         LOVING FIDELITY

an encounter

        is a strange

         and wonderful thing

presence

one person to another

present

one to another

   life flowing

      one to another

but

we can be together
        and not meet

we can live in the same house day after day
        sit at the same table
        kneel at the same pew
        read the same books
            but never meet

we can kiss
        gestures of love
        apparent tenderness
        but never meet

a meeting is a strange and wonderful thing

presence one person to another
        present one to another
        life flowing one to another

.......but to listen
                    to listen intently
my God i wish i could listen
                    to my brother

listen to his heart beats

listen to those faint...o so faint...
                    calls
                    which are there
                    hidden

under.....i know not why....
                    some sort of fear

listening
                    but instead
                      i have my own ideas
                      and i penetrate
                        destroying
                        harvesting all that is there

to make bread
                      for i
                      for me
                      for myself

i need to talk
        and walk
           with another

i need to express myself
        say things.....

this is a movement of life
        life that is in me
           and needs to flow out....

i must speak.....and dance
        sharing things i love and hate
           my hopes, my joys, my fears, my griefs...
      giving myself
      giving my life
      giving life

a tiny child needs not only food and shelter
but something more...much more....
a feeling of love
that someone cares for him
ready to die for him
that he is really loved
that he is important....precious
and so he begins to live
begins to sense the value of his being

and so it is that life rises in him
and he grows in confidence
in himself
and in his possibilities of life
and of creation

effort

        conceived. . . . .

            born. . .

                and nurtured

                    in love

the miserable man
i treat you as a stranger....
you were born and reared in
squalor...
you are walled in, for you have
no life
in front of you.....no joys to
look
forward to....no loving
children....
no esteem

t
w
o

p
r
i
s
o
n
s

d
i
v
i
d
e
d

b
y

a

g
u
l
f

i, with my clean clothes, my
sensitive nose (i hate bad
smells)
my politeness....a warm
house...
a world of security...the light
of reality does not penetrate my
cell, the reality of human
misery
so widespread, so deep.....

two prisons divided by a gulf: the miserable
man......
and, imprisoned in the cell next door, the man
of means
comfortably installed.....and so the world
goes on,
and the gulf gets wider

who will be the bridge

"i do not want to be reborn

but if that should happen

i would like to find myself amongst the untouchables

in order to share their affliction,

their sufferings

and the insults they are subject to.

in this way,

perhaps i would have the chance

to liberate them and myself

from this miserable condition."

gandhi

two worlds that never meet
divided by a gulf called fear.....

who can assuage this fear

who can heal the wounds of this fear
riches will not bring comfort
to the man without hope....
he needs the warm light of confidence
a will to live....he knows his misery
he is too convinced of his
apparent worthlessness
what he lacks is not knowledge
rather the hope and strength
to rise from the filth.....

where to find this strength
springing from hope
which will conquer fear?

"blessed are the merciful

for they shall obtain mercy"

jesus